eat
sleep
fly

Maryjo Koch's

eat
sleep
fly

A Butterfly's View of Life

**Andrews McMeel
Publishing, LLC**

Kansas City · Sydney · London

Andrews McMeel Publishing, LLC
an Andrews McMeel Universal company,
1130 Walnut Street, Kansas City, Missouri 64106

www.andrewsmcmeel.com

Concept and Design: Jennifer Barry Design, Fairfax, California
Production Assistance: Kristen Hall

12 13 14 15 16 WKT 10 9 8 7 6 5 4 3 2 1

ISBN: 978-1-4494-0988-3

Library of Congress Control Number: 2011932646

Attention: Schools and Businesses
Andrews McMeel books are available at quantity discounts with bulk purchase for educational, business, or sales promotional use. For information, please e-mail the Andrews McMeel Publishing Special Sales Department: specialsales@amuniversal.com

all lives transform . . . and butterflies are nature's most exquisite species inspiring change. Their life cycle is nothing short of miraculous. What could be more symbolic than the moment a butterfly emerges from its chrysalis and takes to the sky?

Butterflies arrive with the flowers each spring. Without them, my garden would not be complete. When I see the first Swallowtail floating from flower to flower, it reminds me that life is a journey of change and rebirth. When I watch a Sphinx moth zip by me, then disappear right before my eyes only to reemerge in front of me, its wings curled and folded to resemble the leaf it was resting on, I can't help but think there is magic in the world.

Nature has generously bestowed an endless array of colors and patterns on the wings of butterflies and moths. I like to preserve their beauty by painting them. I am as entranced when I paint a Sunset moth in its emerald, lavender, crimson, and brilliant yellow boldness as I am when capturing a translucent Clearwing butterfly in watercolor.

With their brief, complex lives, butterflies and moths are dazzling messengers, telling us of the fragility of life, and the possibility of hope.

—Maryjo Koch

All glory comes from daring to begin.

There's nothing about a caterpillar that tells you it's going to become a butterfly.

Change gives us branches

so we can reach new heights.

Necessity makes the timid brave.

To become a butterfly,
you must want to fly so much
that you're willing to
give up being a caterpillar.

Change is less challenging when you get enough sleep.

Every butterfly emerges in its own time.

Quality begins on the inside and then works its way out.

*When you're
ready to fly,
put your best colors
forward.*

Those who seem most fragile are often surprisingly bold.

Butterflies are caterpillars that struggle and come through in flying colors.

Change isn't always rosy— sometimes it comes with a few thorns.

Most of us change,
not because we see
the light,
but because we feel
the heat!

Sometimes change can make you feel blue.

Keep an eye out for new possibilities.

Try different tactics to get where you want to go.

Sometimes the best nectar is hard to get.

The difference between try and triumph is a little "**umph**!"

If you're flying in circles, make a new flight plan.

The greater the challenge,

the greater the rewards.

*Life is a
work in progress,
and we paint a little
of it every day.*

Search for who

you want to become.

*When your
soul sings,
take good notes.*

To be irreplaceable,

always be different.

It's not the days in your life that count, it's the life in your days.

about the butterflies

Cover *Left to right:* Yellow Pansy butterfly *(Junonia hierta)*, African Giant swallowtail *(Papilio antimachus)*, and Essex Emerald moth *(Thetidia smaragdaria)*
Butterflies and moths are symbols of change and transformation in human cultures around the world. From tiny eggs or wriggling caterpillars to magnificently colored, winged adults, they transform with flying colors in one of nature's most thrilling displays!

Butterflies and Flowers *Left to right:* Sulphur Alfalfa butterfly *(Colias eurytheme)*, Common Blue butterfly *(Polyommatus icarus)*, Cabbage White butterfly *(Pieris rapae)*, and California Dogface butterfly *(Zerene eurydice)*
Embodying the spirit of summer, butterflies announce the beginning and end of flower season. Meadow-dwelling butterflies feed on leaves and grasses when they are caterpillars and on flower nectar when adults, and many pollinate flower species as they flutter from stem to stem. Butterflies use their antennae to detect which plants are producing nectar. Analogous to human taste buds, their antennae have chemoreceptors that are used for assessing the environment's physical and chemical properties.

Butterfly Eggs *Clockwise from top:* Single Large White butterfly egg, pair of Dingy Skipper eggs, row of Essex Skipper eggs, single Pale Yellow egg, single Marbled White egg, single Small Copper egg, and cluster of Silver-Washed Fritillary eggs
Female butterflies lay many eggs during their short life span to insure that a sufficient number will survive. Some butterflies lay only one egg at a time; others lay eggs in small clusters, while others lay hundreds at a time. The eggs are usually laid in a protected location on or near the plants that the soon-to-be caterpillars will eat. Most eggs are attached to the plant with a fast-drying glue-like chemical that the female butterfly secretes along with the egg.

Five-Spotted Hawkmoth Caterpillar *(Manduca quinquemaculata)*
Caterpillars are complex animals, carrying within their cells everything necessary to create adult butterflies and moths. As they inch their way through larval life, they must protect themselves against countless predators in an eat-or-be-eaten world. Some sport carnival colors to advertise their poisonous dispositions, while others have spikes, hair, and other tactile warning signs to repel birds or other creatures who might relish a juicy snack. Many are camouflaged to blend into their surroundings and their host plants, thus hiding them from predators.

Caterpillars on Branches
The caterpillar stage of the butterfly's life cycle is a time for growth. Caterpillars, also known as a larvae, spend their time eating and growing. Most live from about two weeks to a month. For many butterflies, this is the longest part of their life cycle.

Puss Moth Caterpillars *(Cerura vinula)*
Found in Europe and North Africa, this caterpillar is named after the cat-like appearance of the adult moth it will become. When disturbed, the caterpillar strikes an unusual, larger-than-life defensive posture: its head rears up and is drawn back into the thorax of its body, causing it to swell and reveal a scarlet collar and two staring false eyes. At the same time, its twin tails curl forward and two red, whip-like filaments called *flagellae* flick wildly from side to side. This dramatic display often wards off unsuspecting predators.

Spicebush Swallowtail Caterpillar and Butterfly *(Papilio troilus)*
Caterpillars have been likened to primitive feeding tubes with feet. In just two weeks of continuous eating after hatching, a caterpillar can reach twenty-seven hundred times its original weight. Also known as the Green-Clouded or Green-Spotted swallowtail, this caterpillar feeds on spicebush and sassafras leaves and wildflowers. While pupating, the young larvae roll themselves up in a folded leaf bound by lines of silk and eat their way to adulthood. Their large black eyespots are not actually eyes at all but protective patterning that makes them resemble formidable garden snakes to hungry birds during the vulnerable larval stage.

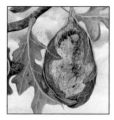

Oak Silk Moth Caterpillar and Chrysalis *(Antheraea harti)*

When a caterpillar is ready to become a butterfly or moth, it spins a silk-like casing called a chrysalis or cocoon around itself and attaches its hind end to a branch. The cocoons of Oak Silk moths resemble soft, white furry eggs. They are made up of a single thread of silk, sometimes a mile in length, spun round and round by the caterpillar. Inside this comfy sleeping chamber, the caterpillar hangs head down as it transforms for the last time to form wings.

Monarch Butterfly Emerging from Chrysalis *(Danaus plexippus)*

When a butterfly finally emerges from its chrysalis, its wings are soft and folded. Once fully emerged, the wings unfold and harden, and the butterfly takes to the sky. The Monarch butterfly, famous for its annual migration—is the only species of butterfly to migrate both north and south, as do birds. However, no single butterfly makes the entire round trip—each migration spans three to four generations. Monarchs are native to North America, ranging from southern Canada to northern South America, but they are found in many other countries around the world. They are one of the few insects capable of making transatlantic crossings.

Comet Moth *(Argema mittrei)*

Also called the Madagascan moon moth, this graceful, slow-flying moth is an endangered native of the rain forests of Madagascar. One of the largest silk moths in the world, it has a wingspan of up to eight inches and two red comet-like tails measuring six inches in length. Comet moth caterpillars pupate inside their silvery silken cocoons for two to six months. The cocoons are the size of chicken eggs and are uniquely adapted to the wet conditions of the rain forest, having a meshlike structure that allows them to drain. Once the adults emerge, they are unable to feed and must subsist on stored lipids acquired during the larval stage. They live for only four to five days, and their lives are devoted almost entirely to reproduction.

California Sister Butterfly, dorsal and ventral sides *(Adelpha bredowii)*

Native to its namesake state, California Sister butterflies are common to the oak-covered hills, groves, and valley streams of California and parts of Mexico and the Southwest. The caterpillars feed on the abundant oak leaves, while adults feed on the rotting fruit and flower nectar of various native trees and woodland shrubs. A California Sister is easy to recognize by the bold black coloring on the dorsal (upper) side of its wings, which is banded with white median stripes. Each of its forewings has large orange spots.

Madagascan Sunset Moth *(Chrysiridia riphearia)*

Widely regarded as one of the most beautiful of all *Lepidoptera*, this large colorful moth was thought to be a butterfly for many years because of its vivid, sunset-colored wings, lack of feathery, moth-like antennae, and because, unlike most moths, it flies about during the day. It is found on the island of Madagascar, and the adult moths prefer to feed on the nectar of white or whitish-yellow flowers found in the tropical forests of the island.

Multicolored Butterflies

There are approximately 265,000 different species of butterflies and moths in the world and only 7.5 percent of them are butterflies. Their wings come in an almost endless array of colors and patterns that serve as camouflage or warning signals to predators while making them attractive to prospective mates. Often, their wings have a totally different coloration on each side, so that as they flutter about in the wild and in our gardens, their wings appear to be constantly changing.

Pipevine Swallowtail *(Battus philenor)*

This swallowtail is a beautiful iridescent black and blue butterfly abundant in North and Central America. It feeds on pipevine plants as a caterpillar, and on the nectar of thistles and woodland flowers as an adult. The upper side of its forewings are black, while the hind wings are brilliant blue. The undersides of its wings are black, with single C-shaped rows of orange spots in a small iridescent blue field on its hind wings. The Pipevine swallowtail is poisonous to predators, and several other species of swallowtail, such as the Eastern Tiger swallowtail, the Eastern Black swallowtail, the Spicebush swallowtail, and the Red-spotted Purple swallowtail, mimic its markings as protection.

Moths and Light

Butterflies and moths vary widely in their sensitivity to light, and are considered to have the widest visual range of any form of wildlife. Moths are positively *phototactic*, meaning that they are attracted to and move towards sources of light. There are numerous theories as to why. One suggests that moths have evolved to navigate and orient themselves in the dark using celestial sources of light. Terrestrial, manmade light sources are very recent on the evolutionary timeline. Moths aren't able to differentiate between the two light sources and often end up flying into lights or open flames because they have no history of dealing with the conflicting signals that can lead to their demise.

Blue Morpho Butterfly *(Morpho rhetenor)*

Bearing a name that means "to change form" in Greek, Blue Morpho butterflies not only change during metamorphosis, but also appear to change colors as adults, depending on the angle at which their wings are viewed. Predators bedazzled by an iridescent Blue Morpho are left perplexed, as it seems to vanish before their very eyes. The brilliant blue wings are brown on their undersides, so when the butterfly alights wings up, poof! It appears to be just another leaf. There are over eighty species of Morpho butterflies. The large, brilliant blue male Morpho *rhetenor* ranges in size from 5 1/2 to 7 inches. Found throughout the forests of South and Central America, these butterflies feed on tree sap and the fluids of rotting fruit.

Wing Eyespots

The large eyespots on the wings of butterflies and moths allow for one of nature's most eye-catching means of escape. Offering colorful targets purposefully positioned away from vital organs, eyespots fool would-be attackers by giving a butterfly the few extra seconds it needs to make its getaway. The colors of butterfly wings come from two different sources: chemical pigmentation and structural color. Structural color stems from the specific composition of the wings, which are covered by thousands of microscopic scales, split into two to three layers. Each scale has multiple layers separated by air. When light hits the different layers, it is reflected numerous times, causing intense and changing colors known as iridescence.

Two-Tailed Pasha Butterfly *(Charaxes jasius)*

With distinctive twin black tails on its striped hindwings, the Two-Tailed Pasha butterfly is a colorful native of Africa, the Middle East, and the European countries bordering the Mediterranean Sea. It has the largest wingspan (four inches) of any butterfly in Europe.

Blue Night Butterflies *(Cepheuptychia cephus)*

Flowers exist thanks to the symbiotic relationship with their pollinators: the flowers encourage butterflies and other creatures to feed on their nectar, thereby inadvertantly spreading their pollen. Flowering plants attract potential pollinators using a variety of wiles, including color, scent, size, shape, texture, temperature, and motion. Butterflies are especially attracted to red, yellow, orange, pink, and purple blossoms that are flat-topped or clustered and have short flower tubes. The Blue Night butterfly is found throughout the rain forests of the upper Amazonian regions of South America. The dorsal side of its wings is a bright, iridescent blue edged in black. The ventral side is zebra-striped in blue and black.

Orange-Barred Sulphur Butterfly *(Phoebis philea)*

The different genders of many species of butterflies often have very different markings and coloration. As with birds, males tend to be more colorful than females in order to attract mates. But there are also differences of coloration within the same gender. Orange-Barred Sulphur females vary in color depending on the season, having a whitish coloration during the wet season and yellow to orange during the dry season. Males are bright yellow year-round, bearing broad orange bars on their forewings. Butterflies can identify each other by their ultraviolet markings. The coloration of male and female Sulphur butterflies also differs in ultraviolet reflectivity, with the males being strongly reflective and the females non-reflective.

Clearwing Butterflies *(Haetera macleannania)*

One of the differences between butterflies and moths is their antennae. Butterfly antennae are thicker or clubbed on the tips. Moth antennae can vary from straight and thin to plumed and feathery. Near the base of a butterfly's antennae is an important organ used for balance and orientation during flight. With an antenna missing, butterflies are unable to fly in a particular direction and end up flying in circles.

Atlas Moth *(Attacus atlas)*

With a wingspan of between ten to twelve inches, the Atlas moth is one of the largest moths in the world, and is found throughout Southeast Asia. Its name in English is thought to be derived from either the Greek god Atlas, who supported the world on his shoulders, or from the map-like patterns on its wings. However, its name in Chinese means "snake's head" after the snake-like appearance of the markings on its upper wing tips.

Painted Lady Butterflies *(Vanessa cardui)*

The aptly named Painted Lady butterfly wears splashes and dots of colors on its wings. The mottled colors look much like military camouflage, providing effective cover from potential predators. Adult Painted Ladies feed on the nectar of many plants, including thistles, asters, cosmos, blazing stars, ironweeds, and joe-pye weed. The caterpillars feed on a variety of host plants, particularly thistle, mallow, and hollyhock. Painted Ladies can be found on every continent except Australia and Antarctica, and are the most widely distributed butterfly in the world.

Butterfly Eyes *Clockwise from upper right:* Marsh butterfly, Owl butterfly, *Parides photinus* butterfly, Clouded Sulphur butterfly, Green Hairstreak butterfly, *Symbrenthia hippoclos* butterfly, and *Melicita deione* butterfly

Butterflies have two different types of eyes, single and compound. The one pair of single-chambered eyes, called *ocelli*, are primarily for determining the brightness of light and are unable to focus on an individual object. The compound eyes are multifaceted and are used mainly eyesight. Butterflies are able to see light wavelengths from 254 to 600 nm, which includes ultraviolet light, a light that humans are unable to see.

Choir Lacewing Butterfly *(Cethosia biblis)*

Also known as Drury's Red Lacewing, this butterfly's common name comes from the beautiful lacy edging and intricate pattern on the underside of its wings. The rows of black and white markings that run along the center of its wings resemble the faces of a choir, some singing more exuberantly than others. It is found throughout Asia, from Nepal and India, to Central China, Indonesia, and the Philippines.

Endangered Species Butterflies *Left to right:* Large Blue butterfly, Large Copper butterfly, Corsican swallowtail butterfly, Zebra swallowtail butterfly, Regal Fritillary butterfly, Spanish moon moth, Queen Alexandra's Birdwing butterfly, and Homerus swallowtail butterfly

Like the proverbial canary in a coal mine, butterflies and moths are sensitive gauges of environmental conditions. Today, as the world's most adaptable creatures, they are struggling to cope with the impact of human activity on nature. Uncontrolled industrial and urban development, not to mention pesticide use, kills insects in droves. Many species are either threatened, endangered, or, lamentably, extinct. Because they are such a vital link in the chain of all life on earth, from pollination to food, trouble for butterflies means trouble for us all.

Peacock Butterfly, Chrysalis, and Caterpillar *(Inachis io)*

Adult Peacock butterflies are native to the British Isles and are particularly long-lived, many surviving into the winter by hibernating in hollow trees or crevices in bark or stone. They come out of hibernation in March and are among the first butterflies to herald the spring.

Butterflies instill in us a wonderful sense of transformation and hope. The life of a butterfly is a journey of stages and rebirth which can symbolize the changes in our own lives. It is easy to understand why we find them so inspiring.

eat, sleep, fly

The Eight-Fold Path to Butterfly Self-Realization

1. The egg hatches and the newborn larva, or caterpillar, emerges.

2. The soft-bodied caterpillar reflexively searches for safety with its simple eyes.

3. As its outer surfaces harden, the caterpillar eats its eggshell for a first meal, then feeds voraciously on its host plant thereafter.

4. The caterpillar prepares to pupate by shedding its larval skin and forming a chrysalis sack around itself.

5. The caterpillar enters a resting stage inside its chrysalis and industriously reorganizes its entire physical structure, literally dissolving old muscles and legs and replacing them with new legs and wings.

6. The chrysalis splits and the winged adult slowly works itself free, head first.

7. The butterfly extends its soft new wings to allow them to dry and harden. It takes its first flight, developing its mature adult coloration within minutes or days, depending on the species.

8. Males seek out and court females for mating; once mated, the females lay the next generation of eggs on a host plant.